FACES OF THE HOLOCAUST:

MARCEL JABELOT

FACES OF THE HOLOCAUST:

MARCEL JABELOT

BARBARA P. BARNETT

*Translation of Marcel Jabelot's testimony
by Carole Kenney*

Foreword by Ruth Kapp Hartz

FEATURING READER'S GUIDE,
SPEECHES, LETTERS
AND SELECTED REFERENCES

Beach Lloyd

PUBLISHERS
LLC

WAYNE, PENNSYLVANIA

Beach Lloyd Publishers LLC, November 2004

Barnett, Barbara P.
Visages de la Shoah: Marcel Jabelot by Barbara P. Barnett

ISBN: 0-9743158-7-7
Printed in the United States of America
Library of Congress Control Number: 2004112100

Cover design by Kevin Bugge and Dave Moore
Book design by Joanne S. Silver
Technical Director, Ronald Silver
Unattributed photographs are from the author's files.

Cover: *Marcel Jabelot in the Luxembourg Gardens, Paris*

To George,
with appreciation and affection

CONTENTS

Comprehension Questions

ILLUSTRATIONS

TESTIMONIALS

Marcel Jabelot, Holocaust survivor, ended his testimony by saying that the moment one stops respecting another, the danger of Nazism slips in, with the horrors that he himself survived.

Albert Valdman, Professor of French,
Indiana University and Hidden Child

Fifty years after the event, Marcel Jabelot's testimony reveals the terrible presence of the Holocaust in the daily lives of its victims. His reflections are both simple and profound.

Patrick Henry, Professor Emeritus
Whitman College

Jabelot's account [. . .] demands of us today that we attempt to present and explain it to the new generations.

Jacques Adler, Historian and Professor
University of Melbourne
The Jews of Paris and the Final Solution:
Communal Responses and Internal Conflicts, 1940–1944

Jabelot's Holocaust parley is very insightful and adds a highly articulate and original voice to the Shoah[1] testimonies.

Eric Nooter, former Historian and Archivist
American Joint Distribution Committee, Inc.

Very impressive! Abe Plotkin,
Pennsylvania Holocaust Education Task Force,
Concentration camp liberator and
Legion of Honor recipient, June 4, 2004.

---

[1] Shoah: the Hebrew word for the Holocaust.

The speaker is clear, his story gripping, and his deliberate French is excellent for a language class.

> Nelly Trocmé Hewett, daughter of
> Pastor André Trocmé (Le Chambon-sur-Lignon)

The poignant story is told in such a sensitive way that one cannot help but understand [. . .].

> Rosanne L. Simon, French Teacher
> St. Anne's-Belfield School, Virginia

With this testimony, one can never say that it [the Shoah] did not happen!

> Judith Speiller, former Head of the Language Program
> Edison Township (NJ) Public Schools

I was deeply affected by his emotional testimony, but perhaps more so by the strength with which he carried on his life after such suffering.

> Elise O'Connell, *Main Line Life* (July 18, 1996)
> and former student of Barbara P. Barnett

Monsieur Jabelot is a remarkable man who, despite the ordeals he suffered, found peace and *joie de vivre*.

> Charline Einstein, wife of Hidden Child
> Ernst Einstein (Clermont-Ferrand)

FOREWORD

Having known Marcel Jabelot personally, it is at once "easy" and "difficult" to introduce this book that is dedicated to him. "Easy" to speak of his tireless work to ensure that the dark years of the Shoah are never forgotten, "difficult" because there is so much to say about Marcel Jabelot in a few words.

Having been a Hidden Child in Vichy France, I had the good fortune of spending precious hours with Marcel during my many trips to Paris, and during his visit to the United States in 1996 for the premiere of Barbara Barnett's superb film, *Visages de la Shoah*, on which this book is based.

Despite terrible suffering in death camps, the loss of his entire family, and a difficult recuperation after the War, Marcel Jabelot had a warm and noble personality, was elegant in mind and body, and won the hearts of those who came to know him. This charisma allowed him to speak with conviction in numerous high schools, junior high schools and colleges. My own experiences differ considerably from his, but the book about my hidden childhood (*Your Name is Renée*) also represents a side of the Holocaust that complements Marcel Jabelot's story.

There are few survivors who have done so much to perpetuate the Memory of the Shoah, and to devote their adult life to this cause, as did Marcel Jabelot. He was an activist, an educator, a witness and a source of support for those of lesser strength and courage.

This book is a continuation of Marcel's work of Bearing Witness and, for years to come, will certainly become a reference for students studying the Holocaust.

In our struggle for a better world, memories are our most powerful weapons. May the words of Marcel Jabelot be forever engraved in our minds:

> "Oblivion ought not to enshroud anew
> those who did not return." [2]

Ruth Kapp Hartz
August 6, 2004

---

[2] Quoted from Marcel Jabelot's Legion of Honor acceptance speech.

PROLOGUE

Thanks to the Centre de documentation juive contemporaine in Paris, I had the good fortune to meet French Holocaust survivor Marcel Jabelot in 1993 and gather his moving testimony. Toni Banet videotaped our conversations with talent and patience, and I am very grateful to her. I would also like to thank the National Endowment for the Humanities for the grant that allowed me to travel to France, conduct interviews and research valuable records. Likewise, the Agnes Irwin School, where I have taught for more than three decades, has generously helped me with both financial and moral support.

After returning to France a second time to speak with Marcel Jabelot about life after Auschwitz and using the unedited interviews with my students, I produced the video *Visages de la Shoah: Marcel Jabelot [Faces of the Holocaust: Marcel Jabelot]* with Martha G. Lubell and Sharon Mullally. It received Honorable Mention in the Jewish film competition at the Judah Magnus Museum in Berkeley, California, aired on Free Speech TV, was featured on National Public Radio, and shown at professional conferences in France and the United States.

In 1996, Marcel Jabelot and his lovely wife Danièle, whose kindness and friendship I value greatly, traveled to Rosemont, Pennsylvania for the premiere of *Visages de la Shoah* at the Agnes Irwin School. Marcel first spoke to more than two hundred attendees, then to my students in their language classes. The students, who had already written to this courageous Holocaust survivor, were overwhelmed by the possibility of speaking with him in person. One of these young women said, "For me, Marcel Jabelot will always be the face of the Holocaust."

In keeping with my mission as "guardian of Memory," I have published this book that includes the text of the film as well as other resources for teachers and students. I will be eternally grateful to Marcel Jabelot, an extraordinary man and dear friend, who generously agreed to share his moving testimony with me and with hundreds of students. I would like his story to remain alive so that no one ever forgets. Although he died too soon in 1999, I hope my efforts will help perpetuate his memory and that the words "never again" will remain with us forever.

Barbara P. Barnett

Danièle Leclercq Jabelot and Marcel Jabelot in Villanova, 1996. Photo by Harry Hartz

INTRODUCTION

Marcel Jabelot was born on May 31, 1924, to a working class father from Poland and a Parisian mother. After the German invasion of France, he and his family moved to the Free Zone in Nice where he secretly began medical studies.

He was arrested in September 1943 with his mother, father and paternal grandmother (78 years old), transferred to Drancy and deported to Auschwitz-Birkenau in October 1943, on Convoy #61. His mother and grandmother were gassed upon arrival while his father "disappeared" a month later. Marcel Jabelot spent nearly eighteen months at Auschwitz-Birkenau and miraculously survived the Death March in January 1945.

Despite the loss of his entire family (a total of sixteen members), tuberculosis and the theft of all his possessions, he remade a life for himself after the War: a successful career in business and a happy marriage. Marcel Jabelot retired at the age of sixty, in order to study history, economics and sociology at the Sorbonne, and to speak to school students about the Holocaust. In March 1995, he was decorated Chevalier in the Legion of Honor. He died on March 23, 1999, at the age of seventy-four.

Georges and Simone Jablonowicz, Marcel's parents

Marcel Jabelot at 19, with his mother in Nice.

INTERVIEWS WITH MARCEL JABELOT
BY BARBARA P. BARNETT
(1993–1994)

PART ONE

1) THE GERMAN OCCUPATION

So as I was just telling you, I was born in Paris of Polish descent. I went to school in Paris and, at the beginning of the war, I had just started medical studies. And then when the Germans came, when France lost the war and the Germans came into Paris—when they invaded and occupied France—we left for the south of France and went to Nice. Why did we go to Nice? Because the Italians had been occupying Nice, and they were much more liberal regarding the Jewish question than the Germans, and they were better even than the French. And then, at a certain point—in September 1943—the Italians stopped fighting. They signed an armistice and they left the Riviera, and the Germans arrived immediately afterwards.

There was no longer a Free Zone?

There was no longer a Free Zone.[3] The Free Zone was abolished in November '42. And as soon as the Gestapo[4] arrived in Nice, they began to arrest Jews. There were many Jews in Nice because they were well treated by the Italians,

---

[3] The part of France not occupied by the Nazis in the early War years (1940–1942).
[4] Nazi Secret police.

who were not anti-Semitic. And when the Gestapo arrived, they began to arrest Jews *en masse*.

France in 1942, the Occupied Zone to the north and the "Free" Zone to the south.
(Map adapted from Idrac 2004, 89)

2) THE ARREST OF MARCEL JABELOT

That was when we were arrested. I was arrested around September 25 or 26, 1943, in Nice, along with my father who was 41, my mother who was 39, and my grandmother who was 78 years old. The Gestapo arrested us in our apartment.

How did they know that you were there?

Well, certainly we were denounced. We were definitely denounced.

By French people?

Very definitely by French people. There were a lot of denunciations, because I don't see how the Germans could have known how to identify Jews, if they didn't have outside help. They didn't know where Jewish people lived, where they were, how many there were...they couldn't know. They had to have clues. The Germans either had denunciations by French people or lists that the French police, the French administration, gave them. Because, unfortunately, the French police helped the Germans a great deal. Sadly, the truth must be told! The French police arrested a large number of Jews—mostly foreigners—and later, even French Jews. And then they turned them over to the Germans. That's also historical fact.

**Second massive arrest of Jews in Paris
August 29, 1941.** © BHVP / Fonds France-Soir

3) DRANCY

So, we were arrested, and then we were taken from Nice to Drancy; Drancy is near Paris. Drancy was an internment camp where there were only Jews, of course—women, children, sick people, and babies. There were all categories of people, a majority of foreign Jews, but there were also quite a number of French Jews. We didn't work at Drancy. We just did little jobs—what the French call *corvées*, or chores—small jobs such as sweeping the courtyard, doing the cooking, cleaning. They didn't amount to much. The food was adequate. But we were prisoners; that isn't freedom, is it? And every week, even several times a week, the Germans assembled people to be deported.[5] They were generally convoys of a thousand people—women, children,

---

[5] Sent to a concentration camp.

old people, sick people. Each time the convoy was made up of a thousand people. And we left Drancy October 26–October 27, 1943.

Drancy Internment Camp, the Gate
Ministère de la Défense, Collection D.M.P.A.

4) THE TRAIN TO AUSCHWITZ[6]

The train was made up of freight cars; they weren't passenger cars, they were freight cars. On the floor there was straw. Normally, these cars were used for military transport, and each car was meant to hold forty people. We were about a hundred people per car. In the cars there were women, children, babies, old people, sick people... There was straw

---

[6] Concentration camp in Poland.

on the floor; in a corner of the car, there was a barrel for a toilet. The train must have had about ten cars that transported about a thousand people. The train was guarded by German SS.[7] So we left Paris, and then we began that trip. We didn't know where we were going. We were told, "You will stay with your families. You are going to Poland to work on farms, in agricultural enterprises." We didn't know. But they told us, "You will stay with your families. You will stay together. Don't worry, you are going to work. If you work, there won't be any problems."

We remained on the train for one night and two days. It was already the month of October, and it was beginning to get cold. There were sick people, old people, people who were afraid, babies crying, and there was no way to get comfortable. We couldn't get situated comfortably, and also there were a lot of people who were thirsty, people who were hungry, and there was this whole mixed group of people. The situation was already tragic. We felt that something awful was about to happen; then the train stopped and we arrived at Auschwitz-Birkenau.

5) ARRIVAL AT AUSCHWITZ

You know that the concentration camp of Auschwitz is in Auschwitz (Poland) and three to four kilometers[8] from there, there is another concentration camp, an annex, called Birkenau. At Birkenau all the prisoners were Jewish. So we arrived there, very early in the morning; it must have been 5 or 6 o'clock in the morning. The SS opened the door of the cars and they began to make us get out, and then we heard shouting in German. The SS spoke to us in German and not everyone understood German. Then they hit us with rifles to make us get out faster. There were dogs barking. Well, all that was absolutely horrible. And we had to jump out of the

---

[7] Military Nazi police, originally created in 1925 as Hitler's personal guards, later charged with surveillance of the concentration camps.
[8] one kilometer = 0.6 miles

car. The car was high and there were no steps to walk down. We had to jump. Well, for old people to jump from the car...a woman with her baby can't jump from the car. So there were people who were jumping off, who were falling on top of one another. It was horrible!

Finally, then, we got out of the train and they put us in rows—men on one side, women and children on the other—and then we began to walk like that, and at the very end of the platform there were German officers, very young, too, who must have been 25 years old, very well dressed, almost smiling. I didn't see my mother or my grandmother again; I stayed with my father. And so that's how we entered the camp at Birkenau. It was very cold because at that time in Poland it must have been around -25 or -28 degrees Celsius.[9] It was very cold.

They made us run toward a building where they told us, "Get undressed! You're going to take a shower." We got undressed and, once undressed, we were colder. We took a shower. Afterwards, they made us go outside, completely naked, to run from one barrack to another. Completely naked! It was horrible. And they told us, "Leave your clothes here. You'll get your clothes back soon."

6) TATTOOING A NUMBER

We arrived in another barrack. There they shaved the hair off our entire bodies. It was pathetic; We didn't even recognize ourselves! Imagine if they cut off your hair everywhere—here, there, from your whole body. And once again they made us go outside—still completely naked—and we passed in front of other detainees who had already arrived there before us, other prisoners who were dressed in striped outfits[10]—pajamas—, were sitting on stools, and we

---

[9] Fahrenheit = 9/5 Celsius (Centigrade) + 32
[10] Uniforms of the deportees.

had to pass by them with our left arm held out, and they tattooed a number on our arms, a number like this one.

You still have the numbers?

You see? They tattooed us. It was a horrible scene. Tattooing a number. Then we understood immediately that we were completely losing our identity. We were no longer individuals, we were numbers. They made us leave the barrack again—still stark naked—to go to another barrack, and there they distributed clothing to us. They were striped pajamas, they weren't wool clothes. They were clothes made of an artificial fiber, which didn't keep you warm at all.

7) THE FIRST NIGHT

They made us go into a barrack where there were wooden beds stacked one on top of the other, with three levels (three or four levels). Each bed had a straw mattress with a cover, and that's where they made us sleep. And then the first night, they woke us up in the middle of the night. They shouted, "Get out! Get out! Wake up! Wake up!" So they woke us up in the middle of the night. We were very tired, terrified; we were very scared. They made us go out into the courtyard at night. It was even colder, and we stayed there for a half-hour, standing still. We waited. And then they said, "You can go back in." Again we returned to the barrack, went to bed, slept another two hours and they came back. "Wake up! Get out! Get out!" Three times they did that during the night. We were dead tired. They did all that to frighten us, to condition us psychologically. To create fear.

8) THE FOOD

I was still with my father. They began to give us food. The first food they gave us was soup, soup made with rutabagas. It's what you give to pigs. It's not potatoes, it's not vegetables, it's not carrots, it's food you give to pigs, which had no nourishment, no vitamins, nothing. I remind you that I was nineteen years old when I was deported. So I was still growing. I needed sugar, milk, meat, and fruit. So that was the first food they gave us. The food in the concentration camps wasn't nourishing; it was so inadequate that when I returned from deportation, I weighed thirty-five kilos.[11] What did the food consist of? Soup, a small piece of bread and, in the morning, what they called coffee. It was black water, but it wasn't coffee. And a small piece of margarine; and from time to time, a little piece of sausage.

9) BIRKENAU

So we stayed at Birkenau for a few days, my father and I, and next they sent us to another camp seven or eight kilometers from there—a mining camp. It was next to a coal mine. It was a camp that didn't have many people; there were perhaps five to six hundred persons there, only men. The women were in another camp; they weren't in the mining camp where we were working.

I want to be clear about my mother and my grandmother. I found out one or two months later that, at the time of our arrival, all the women who had been put aside into one group had been immediately sent to the gas chamber at Birkenau. They were gassed almost upon arrival. Of the one thousand people who made up our convoy when we arrived, I believe only about five hundred of us entered [the camp]. And the five hundred others never did; they were immediately gassed. The tragedy is that not everyone got into the concentration camp; extermination took place upon arrival because, of the one thousand people, only half entered. I'm speaking of my convoy. There are convoys where no one went into the camp; they were immediately put to death. The

---

[11] one kilo(gram) = 2.2 pounds

entire convoy was exterminated because sometimes at Auschwitz, there wasn't enough room. And when there wasn't enough room, the Germans didn't complicate the operation for themselves. They immediately exterminated the people who were coming in. That was the system.

10) THE COAL MINE

So, let me go back… My father and I were in this mining camp and they started sending us into the mine to work. I had never known what a coal mine was. You know, it's something dreadful, working in a coal mine. To give you a few technical details… First of all, this mine had been closed before the war because it was dangerous, and the Germans opened it during the war and sent Jews to work in it.

I worked in that coal mine for several months. It must have been November, December, January, until February 1944. In the meantime, my father was sent to another camp. I never heard anything about my father again. I don't know what happened to him. I never had any news of him. As for myself, I was very lucky: they took me out of the mine and put me in a carpentry workshop.

11) THE BELGIAN ARCHITECT

So, I found myself alone in the camp. Luckily, my father had met a Belgian Jew there who was an architect, who was from Brussels,[12] and my father had said to him, "If I'm separated from my son, watch out for him; take care of my son." Thanks to that Belgian architect who looked after me, who helped me, who protected me in a way, I was able to leave Auschwitz alive.

---

[12] The capital of Belgium.

Did he also survive?

He survived too. He's now in Israel and he's 82 or 83 years old. He was able to help me because he had a function in the camp. The Germans needed an architect and they used him as an architect. Because he had a function, he had a better position. You know, in a camp, it was a small society. You had people who were useful [to the Nazis], who worked in the kitchen, who worked as architects, who worked as electricians. So, those who served a purpose were already in a better situation. They weren't beaten. In the camps there were constant beatings; they beat you and beat you—for nothing, for no reason. The whole concentration system consisted of shouting and beatings and hunger.

So I worked in that camp until January 1945. I had arrived there in October '43 and I stayed almost eighteen months. And in January '45 the Russians were approaching. They launched a great offensive from the Polish side, and we could already hear the cannon of the Soviet army.

12) THE DEATH MARCH

And that's when the Germans began to be afraid. They decided to evacuate the camp and to go toward the center of Germany and take all the prisoners with them. What history calls the Death March began on January 18, 1945, to be exact. Why? Because the Germans, when they evacuated the camps, began to make us travel on foot. And in January '45 at Auschwitz, the temperature was terrible—very, very cold. We were all very tired already because it was the end of our concentration camp ordeal, so we were already exhausted. I could barely walk. I was very, very tired. Everyone was like that. I remind you that at that time I weighed thirty-five kilos [seventy-seven pounds].

Circumstances could not have been worse, and the Germans made us march in our desperate state. Anyone who couldn't walk, anyone who fell, a soldier would come immediately and fire a bullet into his head. They didn't want to leave anyone behind. As soon as someone slowed down or couldn't walk anymore, he immediately had a bullet in the head.

So we walked. Many people stayed behind because they couldn't walk. We walked for a day, a night, another day. We had to walk one night and two days. But at some point, the Germans felt that the Russians were arriving quickly, and they wanted to go faster. They saw that we couldn't move fast enough on foot. They made us climb onto a train—not into normal cars, but into open metal cars, the kind that are normally used to transport coal. So they made us get into those open cars. Remember that in the month of January, 1945, snow was falling. They forced us to get in, and the train began to move. We were packed together tightly, very tightly. We could scarcely move. And the trip began. And at that time it was terrible because we hadn't eaten, we were thirsty, we were cold, we were tired, we were packed together, one next to the other. When people fell, they couldn't get up because we were pressed together, and when people fell they were stepped on. There were many who died on that train.

We spent one long night on the train; then it stopped. They made us get off the cars and we began to walk again. Those who survived—because there were many who died during that trip—those who survived began to march, and the Germans led us into a small forest. The exact name of that forest is Egersfeld, I still remember. We walked and walked, dragging one foot in front of the other.

Still in Poland?

It was still in Poland, still in Poland. And then, it was afternoon. It must have been 4 or 5 o'clock. The snow was falling, and then suddenly the Germans told us to stop.

We stopped. We were completely exhausted, and when we had barely stopped, the Germans began to turn toward us with their machine guns, and they shot at us. Thousands died there. I fell to the ground and pretended to be dead. I didn't move. The snow covered me. I didn't move. I saw dead people all around me, people shouting, wounded. I didn't move. When I couldn't hear anything more, saw no Germans and heard nothing, I got up and there were no more Germans. And all around me there were piles of dead bodies; the snow had already covered them. There were people who were shouting. I began to walk in that forest; I became crazy, I was afraid—and then I realized the miracle of having escaped from all that.

13) THE POLISH WOMAN

We were machine-gunned in the forest, but there were five or six of us who had survived. We began to run. We didn't know where to go. And we walked a long time in that forest, and then we noticed a farm. We decided to go to the farm and take refuge in the barn. So we climbed into the barn. We stayed there and we slept in the barn that night. We didn't move because we didn't know if the Germans were still in the village. We were afraid, and we also feared that the people of the farm would see us and find us there, and perhaps report us to the Germans. But we were so tired and so afraid that we didn't want to move.

And in the morning, we decided anyway that one of us who spoke Polish would go down from the barn to speak with the people of the farm, take the risk because we were tired and very hungry. It was our only chance. We had to take that risk.

And one of us who spoke Polish well, a Polish Jew (we were all Jews) went down. He went to talk to the peasants, and we were very lucky. The peasant was a woman, an old woman with her daughter. Right away they brought us food, soup, clothing. We were very lucky; these people did not turn us over to the Germans.

But she told us, "Don't move from the barn, because the German police are still circulating in the village, checking, and if you're found there, you'll be shot immediately, and me too. I'll be shot because I let you stay here." So we stayed there and finally we were able to eat properly—well, almost. For us, it was extraordinary to have bread, to have soup, nourishing hot food, and to have warm clothes, warm socks, woolen socks, a sweater. It was extraordinary.

14) THE RUSSIANS

Then forty-eight hours later, the Russians—the Soviet army—arrived. The Russian army picked me up. I got very sick due to vitamin deficiencies. I remind you that I was still growing then, and that I hadn't had the normal vitamins that I should have had, and I fell ill. My legs were paralyzed, and the Soviet army hospitalized me in Krakow.[13] I was well cared for, too. I stayed there until the end of February 1945. Then I left the hospital, and at that time the war was still going on. Remember that the war ended only in May; this was February 1945.

I was in Krakow. There were many prisoners of war, English and French. Everyone who had been liberated by the Soviet army found themselves there while waiting to return home. But since the war wasn't over yet, we couldn't go home. We stayed there, waiting.

At that time, there was no French delegation as yet, so no one could take care of us. The Russians assembled us in Polish Army barracks[14] in Krakow and there were thousands of people in those barracks. Hygiene wasn't very good, and typhus had broken out in certain rooms. It was very dangerous, especially because I was in a very weakened condition. If I got typhus, I would die right away.

---

[13] City in Poland.
[14] Housing for soldiers and detainees.

15) THE RED CROSS

I was very lucky, because I went to the Polish Red Cross where there was a woman, a Polish woman, who had lived in Paris for a long time, and spoke French very well. She told me, "You have to leave Krakow because you have to rejoin the French authorities as quickly as possible in order to have French protection." So I asked her, "But where are the nearest French authorities?" She told me that the closest, the nearest French authorities, were in Rumania, in Bucharest.[15]

Well, I don't know if you realize it, but on a map Krakow is here and Bucharest is there; you cross all of Eastern Europe. I was all alone, and I had no money. I had no car. It was wartime. I was twenty years old and I didn't speak Russian and I didn't speak Polish.

So what did you do?

Well, you know, when you are very young, you do foolish things. I wouldn't do it again now, because I think. When one reflects too much, one does nothing. That is the great lesson of life: too much thinking paralyzes—a great lesson. Well, I said to that woman, "Listen, if you tell me to leave, I'll leave." And so I did. I left Krakow and went to Slovakia in the south of Poland, to Czechoslovakia. Then I went through Hungary, and there again I was very lucky. I fell upon an American organization called the "JOINT,"[16] and they helped me.

16) BUCHAREST-ODESSA-MARSEILLE

They transported me to Bucharest. In Bucharest they already had a French embassy, so I immediately had French papers.

---

[15] Capital of Rumania.

[16] The American Joint Distribution Committee, created in 1943 to help the Jews.

You decided to return to France?

Well, I decided to return to France because I wanted to find my family. I had no news about my father or my mother. You know that in my family, there were sixteen people who were deported. I was the only one who returned, out of sixteen people. Aunts, cousins, grandfather...sixteen people!

So I found myself in Bucharest. I decided to return to France to try and see if I could find someone from my family. The French embassy took me to Odessa[17] in Russia, and in Odessa the Russians put us on a British ship—a British troop transport—which took us from Odessa to Marseille. And I arrived in Marseille on May 3, 1945.

17) POST- WAR

When did you find out that your whole family was dead?

Well, I found out when I returned to Paris, and when I waited and no one came back. I am the only one who returned. Unfortunately, that was the only indication. No one came back. I never had any news about anyone. I don't know under what conditions they died, where they died, when they died. I never knew how my father died, nor my grandfather, my aunts, cousins, uncles. I never found out.

Next, because of the hunger and lack of vitamins, I contracted pulmonary tuberculosis. Tuberculosis is a disease of poverty. I fell seriously ill and at that time, in 1945, they didn't know how to treat tuberculosis. Well, I was very sick, and I was sent to a sanatorium in Switzerland. I was very lucky to have been sent to Switzerland, because in Switzerland there was no problem with food. I had very good doctors and their treatments were successful. So, then I returned from the sanatorium. I had to work because my

---

[17] Port in the former USSR.

parents had left all their things in our apartment, and we had been robbed and looted. I found very few things, very few things.

18) ANTI-SEMITISM

When you were young, in Nice, for example,
or in Paris, was there a lot of anti-Semitism?

Before the war in France there was a lot of anti-Semitism,[18] and there was a lot of xenophobia.[19] There was an influential anti-Semitic press, with anti-Semitic newspapers. There was a newspaper called *Gringoire* (it wasn't a daily paper, it was weekly, printing about 500,000 copies a week). It was openly anti-Semitic. There was a great deal of anti-Semitism in France before the war.

FRANÇAIS ! AU SECOURS !
INSTITUT D'ETUDE DES QUESTIONS JUIVES . 21 RUE LA BOETIE . PARIS .

Anti-Jewish propaganda poster, Paris 1941, posted in the metro by the Institut d'études des questions juives (initiated May 11, 1941).
Bibliothèque Historique de la Ville de Paris / Fonds France-Soir

---

[18] Attitude of hostility against the Jews.
[19] Systematic hostility against foreigners or those who are different.

You know, when the first anti-Semitic measures were taken by the Vichy government of Marshall Pétain,[20] people were indifferent. Beginning in '43—1943—the atmosphere changed. People started to realize the tragedy that befell the Jews, the horrible situation; and then, there were already priests who were hiding Jews. There were French people as well, who began to hide Jews and to help them. That's true. That happened. The truth must be told.

But I think that it was a delayed reaction. Now, in '43 perhaps people also began to believe that Germany was going to lose the war, because Germany was experiencing the first defeats in '43. I don't know. I think that the reaction of the French to protect Jews was late in coming. It was only in '43 that there was a change in atmosphere. That's what I personally believe.

But in the beginning, the French were indifferent. And I repeat, there was very strong anti-Semitism in France before the war. You know, when the Germans arrived, the ground was already very well prepared. My opinion is that Hitler succeeded in finishing the work that had already been started long before. He finished the work. During the Dreyfus[21] affair, anti-Semitism in France rose dramatically. After-wards, anti-Semitism stayed with the people. You know, the Dreyfus affair took place in 1890–1894, but someone who was ten, twelve, fifteen years old then—how old was he in 1940? He didn't forget. Because certain people remained anti-Semitic, minds were prepared. People thought that Jews were dangerous creatures.

But what is more tragic, the conclusion of all that was that the governments of the Western countries knew, and they did nothing.

---

[20] Collaborationist government established in France and led by Marshall Pétain.

[21] French Jewish officer accused and then acquitted of espionage.

PART TWO

19) RETURN TO PARIS

You seem like a happy man. How did you resume your life after Auschwitz?

Well, I seem like a happy man now. You are seeing me fifty years later, fifty years after it all. If you had seen me in 1945, I didn't look happy. First of all, when I came back, I was twenty-one; I was in very bad shape physically because I had just gotten out of Auschwitz, the concentration camps. I weighed about thirty-five kilos [seventy-seven pounds]. And when I returned to France, the greatest tragedy was finding out that my family wasn't there. And the greatest sorrow was finding out that of the sixteen people of my family who were arrested, I was the only one who survived. And that sadness is so great that even today, not a single day goes by that I don't think about my family, and about my parents.

When I returned to Paris from Switzerland, I was all alone; I had no parents, no family, no money. I couldn't resume my medical studies. I had to begin to live all over again. What saved me is that when you are twenty-one years old, you know, everything is much easier. If a thing like that had happened to me at forty, I don't know what I would have done. Maybe I couldn't have withstood it, maybe I would have fallen into depression, and maybe I would have committed suicide. It's possible. But at twenty-one, you know, life goes on. And then I also have to point out that it was post-war France, during the period of Liberation. France had been occupied for four years, four years where people were afraid. It was a very difficult occupation, especially for Jews. So afterwards, when we returned, it was the Liberation. Then, everyone wanted to live, everyone wanted to have fun. At twenty-one, obviously, life prevails, you see?

20) WORK

And then I looked for work. I learned the real estate business. And I became a competent specialist. And afterwards, when I had learned the business, I earned a good living. I said, "There's no point in remaining an employee; I'll start my own company." And with a friend, we started a company and I worked for myself in my own company. I became my own boss. And I worked in that company until I was sixty.

So, that was successful, and I always said that if I had the chance at sixty years of age and had the means to stop working, I would retire. Because, in reality, the true personality always returns. Your personality always prevails; it always returns to the surface. Actually, I was never a businessman. I never had a business mentality. I was forced, I had to earn a living, but I was never a businessman.

I always thought about going back to school, but I knew that, unfortunately, to resume studies, you had to have the means. I knew very well that I wasn't going to return to study Medicine. It's very long, and very specialized. And don't forget that at Auschwitz I lost a great deal of memory. I lost the intellectual means, at twenty-one, with all the problems caused by malnutrition, and my brain cells no longer had the same power that they would have had if I had been a normally nourished boy. So, I knew very well that I no longer had the same intellectual abilities, and I couldn't attempt complicated studies.

21) THE SORBONNE

So, I always thought that if, at the age of sixty, I had the means to stop, I would become a student again and I would study what I could. And more luck: at sixty I had the means to do it, and I stopped working and then began another life. I started such a new and different life that I have already forgotten the first life. I forgot business, all that. In my memory, it's completely separate.

What are you studying?

I've been studying history for ten years, especially contemporary history, because I want to understand. I want to try to understand how Auschwitz was possible, how the Holocaust was possible, why I was a victim, why my family was killed only because they were Jews. Why?

What happened in Europe? You must understand one thing: that the Holocaust happened in Europe, in an ultra-civilized continent, and in addition, it happened in Germany, the country that has given us the greatest philosophers, the greatest thinkers, the greatest musicians. In an ultra-civilized country. How was that possible? The great lesson is that neither religion nor culture prevented anything. When you study history, you notice one thing: that all the European elite collaborated with Hitlerism. They did not oppose Hitlerism. That is the thing that must be studied, that is what the historians, the philosophers, the thinkers must study: Why did religion and culture not prevent this tragedy?

So you haven't found any answers?

I'm searching. That's why I continue to study. You see? Hitler found a very favorable situation in which to commit these crimes. Because you had a lot of people who were saying that what was done to the Jews was understandable, because the Jews had killed Christ. They had killed Jesus, so this was punishment.

So, to return to what I was telling you, the tragedy is that neither religion nor culture prevented the Holocaust. In reality it is the failure of religion, the failure of culture.

22) LOSS OF FAITH

Now, we can also ask an important question, which concerns all religions. What did God do at Auschwitz? Where was God? What was he doing when they were burning women and children? While they were gassing women and children, where was God? I'll tell you, when I came back from Auschwitz, my personal conclusion—this only has to do with me, it's my personal response—is that if God exists, he has appalling guilt for having allowed the Holocaust to occur. Because allowing women and children to be burned is terrible. That's the first conclusion. And to believe in God after Auschwitz is very difficult.

And then, there is something else that was horrible for me: when I returned from Auschwitz, after Auschwitz, I no longer trusted human beings. That's the problem: humanity. Humanity was capable of doing that, and allowed it to happen, because people knew about it in 1942. They knew everything. (I'm not going to repeat everything that we've already discussed.)

Has your attitude toward people changed?

Well, you see, the first consequence of all that is that when I got married, I didn't have any desire to have children. I said to myself, if humanity is capable of doing what I saw, it is perhaps capable of doing it a second time. If I have children, they risk being victims of that. It's a lack of trust in human beings. I recognize that.

SAINT-MANDÉ CHILDREN'S HOME (on the outskirts of Paris). Twenty girls and their teacher were arrested on July 22, 1944 and later deported to Auschwitz. None survived.

Ministère de la Défense, Collection D.M.P.A.

23) MARRIAGE

When did you get married?

Well, I met my wife in 1971. And then, I hesitated to marry, because I said to myself, with all that happened to me, I risk making my wife unhappy, because I risk mental instability. There are many people who returned from Auschwitz who became unstable. Some committed suicide, some went crazy, many are still in treatment today for depression, still seeing specialists. Many of them have difficulties. So I hesitated before marrying because I didn't want to make my wife unhappy. But we got married, and it appears to be working. There aren't any problems, and I don't bother her too much with my own problems. And my wife, she understands my situation. We don't talk about that too much because we don't want to live our life in a second Auschwitz. One shouldn't dramatize situations either. I am lucky to have a wife who understands me.

24) BEARING WITNESS

So, to come back to me, to come back to my life, well, that is the philosophical basis of my life. Despite everything, if one has decided to live, one must live. Otherwise, if one wants to continually think about all that, one cannot live. But one must not forget. We can't forget. We must bear witness. That's what I'm doing. For ten years now I've been going to schools. I go to see young people; I testify and reveal the truth. I have even written a narrative, which I gave to you. I want to bear witness because I want people to know. And one thing must also be said: that all those people who did not come back, all those who died without tombs... What is a tomb? It is Memory. If we forget them, it's a victory for Hitler.

Père-Lachaise Cemetery, Paris
(Buna-Monowitz [Auschwitz III])

What is the reaction of young people now?

The reaction of young people is that they are horrified. They can't believe, they can't understand why. They don't understand why. They don't understand, they are horrified. They look at me as if I came from the moon. When I tell them about all that, they have great difficulty believing me. When I tell them that French policemen arrested women and children, when I tell them that French policemen separated mothers from their children, they can't believe it.

When I tell them that I wore the yellow star[22] with the word "Jew" on it when I went to school here in Paris, they don't believe it. They can't believe it. It's unimaginable, but it's true.

---

[22] Jews over the age of six in the Occupied Zone were obliged to wear the yellow star as of May 29, 1942.

You've just celebrated your seventieth birthday.
How do you feel?

Well, look, I'll tell you something. My body is seventy perhaps, but my mind isn't yet seventy. I still feel "young" (we mustn't exaggerate). But really, I feel good physically. I think that to remain young, two things are needed: to have a thirst for life and to keep the ability to become indignant about a lot of things. When one loses the capacity for indignation, one is already old, very old.

25) LESSONS

What do you want to say to young people
who will listen to your story?

The great lesson from the Holocaust is that the minute that one no longer respects one's neighbor, one no longer looks at one's neighbor as a human being, a worthy, respectable person, that is the beginning of Nazism. We must respect others, we must try to understand others. Everyone has problems; we must try to understand. And if a politician begins to take power and wants to discriminate against individuals because one is black, the other is Jewish, the third is a Gypsy, the fourth is Asian—it's the beginning of a dictatorship. It's the beginning of fascism.

I believe that's the advice I would give young people. You shouldn't be aggressive, you shouldn't be mean, you shouldn't be jealous. Friendship is very important; one cannot live without friends. One cannot live without love, and one cannot live without tenderness, without affection. So if you want to receive, you have to give. You see, it is a rather commonplace, down-to-earth philosophy, but you don't have to be a great philosopher to understand that. In any case, that's the lesson.

I tell you, at Auschwitz, when I had someone who gave me a tiny morsel of bread, he saved my life. He saved my life. So in everyday life—thank God, this isn't Auschwitz—instead of giving a little piece of bread, we can give a smile. If you give a smile, that's a big piece of bread.

And that's my story.

SPEECHES: 1995–1997

Tuesday, March 14, 1995
Marcel Jabelot's Decoration as
Chevalier in the Legion of Honor

PRESENTATION BY CHARLES PALANT
Awarded in Paris, at the Pavillon Dauphine

Dear friends, dear comrades,
Dear Marcel,

As with all your friends, I was delighted to learn of your nomination as Chevalier in the Legion of Honor. I cannot tell you how touched I was that you asked me to be your sponsor. [. . .]

[Monsieur Palant pays homage to Marcel Jabelot and reminds us that among the 75,000 Jews deported from France, only 2,500 returned in 1945.]

We are among the three per cent [who returned]. The Vél d'Hiv roundups, those interned at Pithiviers, Gurs and Drancy[23] [. . .] Jews who lived in Belleville, Saint-Paul or the *grands boulevards* of Paris, Nice, Toulouse, Marseille, Lyon, and in the most remote villages, were driven out by members of the Milice, the Gestapo, collaborators and Vichy police. Fewer than three per cent of us returned.

Emaciated, skeletal, our tired bodies floated in civilian clothes. People who wanted to know when they would see

---

[23] Internment camp near Paris, also called the "anti-chamber of Auschwitz" or "anti-chamber of death."

their loved ones assailed us. Every time they looked at us, we saw the same question: Why you and not them? As if we, the three per cent who miraculously survived the nightmare, were not orphans and ourselves "back from the dead."

Do you believe, Marcel, that we were right, two years ago, to denounce these terrible crimes in granite and bronze at the Père Lachaise Cemetery? What would happen to the duty of "remembering"—that you serve so well—if it were limited to the haunting evocation of the catastrophe, calling for compassion for the not-forgotten victims, yet ignoring the truth: the economic basis for the crime, at a time when, for the profit of the same people, the smoke of the crematoriums and the smoke of the blast furnaces were merging?

A little more than a half century ago, the Resistance and its heroes entered into the picture. Isn't the defense of Memory a continuation of what they were fighting for, so that the paths of vigilance and hope might remain open?

By your side, Danièle supports and accompanies you with grace and charm in your activities, permitting you to remain faithful to yourself and to us all.

I must now—with pleasure and not without emotion— pronounce the traditional words:

MARCEL JABELOT, IN THE NAME OF
THE PRESIDENT OF THE REPUBLIC
AND BY VIRTUE OF THE POWERS
CONFERRED UPON US, WE AWARD
YOU THE ORDER OF CHEVALIER IN
THE LEGION OF HONOR.

(Continuation) Tuesday, March 14, 1995

MARCEL JABELOT'S SPEECH
Upon Receiving the Legion of Honor Award

Pavillon Dauphine, Paris

Dear friends, dear comrades,

Thank you, Charles, for these words that move me so deeply. I admire the talent with which you, in a few words, were able to recapture a life full of vicissitudes.

How, at this time, could I not think about my parents, who did not return? How proud they would be this evening! It is to them that I dedicate this prestigious decoration.

If today, I see that my many years of work for Remembrance and my fight for truth are recognized and rewarded, I am delighted. It encourages me to persevere.

I want to share this distinction with "L'Amicale de Buna-Monowitz," which I am honored to preside with you, Charles.

[. . .] Why must we tirelessly bear witness? I could not offer a more beautiful or explicit answer than to read to you this short text of the late, sadly missed André Frossard:

> Misfortune made them the witnesses of the most inconceivable crime ever committed on the face of the earth, and they know that it is their duty to ensure that Memory does not fade, because hatred is just waiting for us to forget.

**Memorial at Père-Lachaise Cemetery, Paris
(Buna-Monowitz [Auschwitz III])**

Hitler almost committed the perfect crime, not only because he almost succeeded, but because he almost succeeded in having it forgotten.

When we go to high schools, middle schools, the Sorbonne, our young listeners avidly long for details. We bring them what they don't find in their history books. We give life to these texts. We fill in the gaps of historians who are sometimes biased or reluctant to speak. The moving letters that I receive from these adolescents are my greatest reward. They write that my testimony has shown them where racism and hatred can lead, that this testimony is an urgent call for them to be vigilant.

But telling one's story is not always easy. In addition to the intense emotion that we feel in remembering our time at Auschwitz, we must ask those that hear us to imagine the unimaginable.

Our stories often make people uneasy or...trouble them. We evoke inglorious times: those times of compromise, passivity and indifference. We unveil the immensity of the crime and the zealots who let it happen. We pose the question: how could that happen in Christian Europe, in the most civilized country, that of great philosophers, musicians and poets? We must explain that the Nazis took advantage of the simmering brew of deadly poisons of xenophobia, of anti-Semitism, of what Jules Isaac called so well the "Teaching of Contempt."

Neither religion nor culture prevented these crimes. But our stories must not be a cry of despair. Certainly, we have seen the ugliest side of humanity—but the most beautiful as well, with Christian rescuers[24] who risked their lives to help a number of us.

No, those who did not return must not be forgotten. The evocation of their Memory, the telling of what happened on the "Planet Auschwitz" must serve as symbolic memorials for the many innocent victims.

---

[24] In French, known as « les Justes ».

When the handful of survivors are no longer alive, historians will take over. Brilliant professors will write about the concentration camp phenomenon. Will they know how to describe what a Holocaust survivor called "the days of death"? Will they tell of our daily sufferings, our most foolish hopes? [. . .]

[. . .] I will not conclude without thanking my wife Danièle for all the help that she has given me, with patience, understanding and devotion during all these years. I know that it was not always easy, and that there were difficult moments. I express to her my deepest gratitude.

Dear friends, the buffet awaits you!

Marcel Jabelot
Tuesday, March 14, 1995

Decoration as Chevalier in the Legion of Honor

April 28, 1996

SPEECH BY MARCEL JABELOT
at the Premiere of *Visages de la Shoah*
at The Agnes Irwin School

Ladies and Gentlemen,

I would first like to thank Miss Penney Moss, Head of the Agnes Irwin School, for allowing this special program to take place.

I turn with emotion toward Mrs. Barbara Barnett, who produced this video. I would like to express to her my gratitude and my warmest congratulations for the remarkable work she accomplished. She gathered my testimony with great sensitivity, much tact and perseverance. It is difficult to interview a Holocaust survivor; you have to take precautions, control the emotions you feel in dealing with such tragic events. Barbara researched archival documents in Paris and in Washington, and created a very successful documentary. Her film will be a very good pedagogical tool; and therein lies its importance.

My thanks to Toni Banet, who held the video camera with the talent of a professional.

I cannot personally thank each student in Barbara's class. How can I describe to you the emotion I felt receiving their letters and their audiocassettes? It is with tears in my eyes that I read and listened to them. I admired their excellent French and their great maturity. I will never forget their touching sensitivity.

I would like to thank all those who contributed to the Holocaust Education Project. You made it possible for this testimony to be shown to American young people. And so, Memory will be safeguarded. It will be a weapon in the ongoing struggle against Holocaust denial.

My testimony is not only a look back at the past, not only a symbolic memorial for my family members who never had one. But it is also, especially for young people, a pressing invitation to think about the respect of human dignity, to understand the tragic results of indifference, cowardice and intolerance. May this film lead to vigilance—that is my greatest wish.

"Never again Auschwitz."

THE PLAQUE AT DRANCY
[The French Republic
in homage to the victims
of the racist and anti-Semitic persecutions
and of the crimes against humanity
committed under the authority of the *de facto*
"Government of the French State"
(1940–1944)
Let us never forget]

July 20, 1997

Speech by Marcel Jabelot in Drancy
for the Day of Commemoration
of Racist and Anti-Semitic Persecutions

Chief of Police,
President of the *Conseil Général*,
Mayor,
Elected officials,
Representatives of religious groups,
Ladies,
Gentlemen,

The CRIF (Conseil représentatif des institutions juives de France [Committee Representing Jewish Institutions of France]) bestowed upon me, as a Holocaust survivor, the honor of representing them on the occasion of this Day of Remembrance of the victims of racist and anti-Semitic persecutions, committed under the authority of the so called "French government" from 1940–1944.

Drancy Memorial: the train car

Fifty-four years ago, on October 3, I arrived here at Drancy, more precisely at the Drancy Internment camp. I was nineteen years old. I was with my parents and my 78-year-old maternal grandmother. We stayed here just under a month. On October 28, 1943, we were deported to Auschwitz- Birkenau. I was the only one who returned from there.

But I am here to remember those days (July 16 and 17, 1942) called the Vél d'Hiv roundup, which the Nazis, with characteristic derision and cynicism, called "Operation Spring Wind."

At 4:00 a.m. on July 16, 4,500 French policemen arrive, with names and addresses in hand, in the neighborhoods where many Jews resided. They knock forcefully on the doors of these modest apartments. The tenants, barely awake, find themselves before these Paris "peacekeepers" and do not understand what is happening to them. They are told to pack a few things as quickly as possible, and that they are being arrested. They are in a state of shock: shouting, crying, begging, fainting. These unfortunate people cannot believe that French civil servants are arresting, with no hesitation, entire families—some sick, some bed-ridden and carried out on stretchers. Women are dragged on the sidewalk...

But who were these people seized by the police as dangerous individuals? Simply, foreign-born Jews who were forced to leave their countries, victims of pogroms and anti-Semitism. They had come to France, for them the country of the Rights of Man, the French Revolution, and the Paris Commune. They felt protected by the French Republic. Their children, born in France, were French citizens. Never would they have believed that the French authorities would turn them over to their declared enemies, the Nazis.

President Jacques Chirac found the right words when he declared on July 16, 1995:

It is difficult to evoke those moments because those dark hours tarnish forever our history and are a blemish on our past and our traditions. Yes, the criminal madness of the Occupier was supported by the French, by the French State. France, country of the Enlightenment, of the Rights of Man, land of welcome and asylum, France that day carried out the irreparable. She gave her charges to their executioners.

During these two days of July 16 and 17, 1942, nearly 13,000 Jews were apprehended: 3,000 men, 5,800 women and 4,000 children. More than fifty Parisian buses took approximately 8,000 people—families with children under sixteen—to the Vél d'Hiv; the others went directly to the Drancy internment camp...

The Prefecture of Police had planned to arrest more than 22,000. It indicates the number reached as 13,000. One must say that some courageous civil servants—with unimaginable risks—had warned friends and neighbors about what was going to happen. Those who were aware of the trap being set for them had to quickly improvise: leave their apartments, give their children to courageous French citizens, remove their yellow stars and go into hiding. One can only imagine the terrible sacrifices and the courage needed during these moments of grave danger.

These French people who warned, who helped, who welcomed and hid young children, those who showed humanity, solidarity, who understood that what was happening was unacceptable, not only saved lives but, in doing so, also saved the honor of France. We call them "the Righteous." Our appreciation is infinite, our gratitude to them immense.

Beginning on July 19, scarcely two days after the roundup, a convoy of adults leaves Drancy for Auschwitz. Their frightened families see them leave toward an unknown destination...

Later, with the consent of Vice-Premier Pierre Laval, the order will come to deport the children as well. They arrived alone at Drancy. How to describe these young children in tears walking in the courtyard of the camp? Very quickly, they will be deported, mixed with adults and gassed upon their arrival at Auschwitz.

I tried to describe to you, with sobriety and without exaggeration, what happened in France during those days. The responsibility of the leaders of Vichy is immense. Of the 77,000 Jews deported from France, of whom 11,000 were children, fewer than three per cent returned. It is from here that most of them left for the extermination camps...

It is fortunate that President Mittérrand inaugurated this national Day of Remembrance, to ensure that Memory be preserved.

For us, survivors of the "planet Auschwitz," it is our sacred duty to remember. Memory, that is the memorial to those who left in smoke, in the skies of Auschwitz. We must do everything to ensure that Memory survives after the disappearance of the last witnesses. This responsibility, whose importance cannot escape you, will fall on future generations.

For young people, these tragic events must show where discrimination, the disappearance of human rights and the lack of respect for others can lead. I invite them to show the utmost vigilance. The old murderous demons remain hidden among many of us. They reappear at the slightest crisis that, as always, provokes the search for scapegoats.

It is through Remembrance that these young people will keep France faithful to her republican traditions of justice, humanitarianism and welcome to those who are persecuted.

**Vél d'Hiv roundup, buses parked
along the Vélodrome d'Hiver, July 16–17, 1942**.
BHVP / Fonds France-Soir

Memorial of the Vél d'Hiv roundup. Ministère de la Défense. Collection D.M.P.A.

Letter One of Three, to a Student

January 31, 1997

Mademoiselle,

I understand that the study of History in textbooks is not enough for you. Indeed, when this teaching can be reinforced by the testimonies of those who were in the midst of the events, students can better imagine that they actually happened, and can better understand the events. And then one can ask the witnesses questions. That's what you did in your letter, and I will try to answer you.

At no moment could I imagine, before my arrest, that I was going to be deported. Of course, I was often afraid. But this fear is overcome when one has the fierce will to survive. My parents never wanted to show me that they, too, were afraid. And I did all that I could to hide my own fear.

In the camp, my constant obsession was to do all I could to return, to see my loved ones again, to tell what I had seen—how so many innocent people had been assassinated.

Yes, I tried to pass on my will to survive to those around me. And in the camp, a comforting word could keep someone alive.

Indeed, as you write in the conclusion of your moving letter, you cannot understand. Simply stated, a "normal" mind cannot imagine such horrors. Especially a young, innocent person such as yourself.

But I ask you to tell those around you what you learned from my testimony, and especially to speak up and answer those who say the Shoah never happened.

Now you know. I am reassured. I know that you will help me in my constant struggle against fading memories.

I wish you a happy life, full of good fortune.

Marcel Jabelot

Letter Two of Three, to a Student

January 31, 1997

Mademoiselle,

It is important to me that you saw the videocassette of my testimony, because it is the youth of today who will ensure that Memory survives and that the innocent victims of the Shoah will never again be forgotten.

I am going to try to respond to the interesting questions that you asked me.

No, I did not return to Auschwitz, which in my mind remains the largest communal gravesite of humanity, where almost all of my family perished. I am afraid that I could not see these places again without feeling a shock of overwhelming grief.

I do not want to return to Germany or Poland. For me, these countries are where too many unimaginable crimes were carried out against people whose only "mistake" was being born Jewish.

No, the Germans did not manage to make me "feel inferior." Moreover, that's what gave me the strength to resist their attempts to break me. Besides, I knew that if I allowed myself to be broken, I would never come out alive.

Regarding God, I do not believe that it is necessary to believe in order to survive. On the other hand, strong moral values, such as respect for others, a strong sense of morality and a certain faith in mankind, seem to me indispensable, in order to give meaning to one's life.

It is now up to you to take over the work of Remembrance. I have complete confidence in you.

I wish you luck and happiness.

Marcel Jabelot

Marcel Jabelot

Letter Three of Three, to a Student

January 31, 1997

Mademoiselle,

I was very touched by your letter, for which I thank you.

I understand very well that you wanted to see the home where your ancestors had been slaves.

Auschwitz, unfortunately, is not a "master's home." It is a real death industry, where more than a million people were killed (including fifteen members of my family), only because they were born Jewish.

You can understand that I do not wish to see the place that will remain in history the disgrace of humanity.

By returning there, I would not feel a sense of "triumph"— to use your expression—but rather a deep sense of agony, an immense sadness; and I don't know if my heart would stand up to the shock.

Yes, Hitler wanted to reduce entire populations to slavery. He was defeated. That is our real victory.

I wish you great success in your studies and much happiness in your life.

Marcel Jabelot

READER'S GUIDE

CHRONOLOGY OF WORLD WAR II

1894–1906   Dreyfus Affair

1939
September 1   Germans enter Poland.
September 3   England, and then France,
                     declare war against Germany.

1940
June 14   Germans enter Paris.
June 18   From London, General de Gaulle
                     calls for Resistance.
June 22   Franco-German armistice;
                     Germans occupy 3/5 of the country,
                     in the North, the Occupied Zone.
June 23   Hitler visits Paris.
July 2   Creation of the Vichy government
                     in the Free Zone.
July 10   National Assembly votes the Third
                     Republic out of existence;
                     hands over power to Pétain.
October 3   First series of anti-Jewish laws.

1941
June 2   Second series of anti-Jewish laws.
June 22   Germany attacks Russia.
July 2   Beginning of the confiscation
                     of Jewish businesses.
August 20–21   Creation of Drancy internment camp.

1942

March 27	First trainload of Jews leaves Drancy for Auschwitz.
April 18	Laval returns to office.
May 29	Jews over six years of age in the Occupied Zone are forced to wear the yellow star.
July 16–17	Vél d'Hiv roundup in Paris of approximately 13,000 Jews, for deportation to Auschwitz.
August 23	Archbishop Saliège of Toulouse condemns deportation of Jews.
November 11	Germans occupy the Southern Zone.
December 11	Jews in the Southern Zone ordered to have the word "juif/juive" on identity cards.
December 19	Laval meets with Hitler.

1943

January 31	Creation of the *Milice française,*[25] with Laval as President.
June 21	Klaus Barbie ("the butcher of Lyon") captures Jean Moulin and other leading Resistants.
September 8	Germans take over Italian-occupied territory in southern France.

1944

April 6	Klaus Barbie raids the home for children in Izieu, outside of Lyon.
June 6	Landing of the Allied Forces in Normandy; D-Day.
June 14	Charles de Gaulle returns to French soil.

---

[25] Pro-Nazi, Vichy French Paramilitary created in 1943 to support the German occupation and Pétain's collaborationist government.

1944

| August 17 | Last convoy leaves Drancy for Auschwitz. |
| August 25 | Liberation of Paris. |

1945

January 18	The Death March.
January 27	Russians liberate Auschwitz.
May 8	Germany surrenders.
July 13–15	Pétain tried and convicted.

1954

| April 14 | Last Sunday in April declared national day of commemoration for the victims and heroes of the deportation. |

1958

| June 1 | Charles de Gaulle becomes President of France. |
| September 28 | Constitution of the Fifth Republic adopted. |

1965

| December 19 | Charles de Gaulle re-elected President of France. |

1970

| November 9 | Death of Charles de Gaulle. |

1971

| April | Release of Marcel Ophul's film *The Sorrow and the Pity.* |

1985

| April | Release of Claude Lanzmann's film *Shoah.* |

1987

May 11–July 4   Klaus Barbie tried in Lyon and
                     sentenced to life imprisonment.

1989

May 25   Paul Touvier arrested in Nice
                     for crimes against humanity.

1993

June 8   Bousquet assassinated while awaiting
                     trial for crimes against humanity.

1994

April 19   Touvier sentenced to life imprisonment.

1995

July 16   President Jacques Chirac apologizes for
                     France's role in the deportation of Jews.

1996

July 17   Touvier dies in prison.

1997

October 1   Bishop Olivier de Berranger asks for-
                     giveness for the silence of the French
                     Catholic Church regarding the
                     deportation of Jews.

Major Events in the Life of Marcel Jabelot

May 31, 1924
Marcel Jabelot is born in Paris.

1937
Bar Mitzvah, synagogue de la rue Notre-Dame-de-Nazareth (Paris).

1941
Passed first *baccalauréat* (Paris).

1942
Passed *baccalauréat* in philosophy (Lyon);
began medical studies (Nice).

September, 1943
Marcel is arrested in Nice with his parents and paternal grandmother, and sent to the Drancy internment camp.

October 27, 1943
Marcel and his family are deported to Auschwitz, Poland in Convoy #61.

January 18, 1945
Death March begins (Poland).

May 3, 1945
Return by boat to France (Marseille) via Odessa.

October 1945–August 1946
Treated for tuberculosis in Leysin, Switzerland.

1971
Marcel Jabelot meets Danièle Leclercq.

March 1983
Marries Danièle Leclercq in Neuilly-sur-Seine.

1984
Begins studies at the Sorbonne—history, economics and sociology; continues until his death fifteen years later.

1993
Inauguration of the monument to the victims of Buna-Monowitz (Auschwitz III) in the Père-Lachaise Cemetery.

1993–1994
Interviewed by Barbara P. Barnett.

March 14, 1995
Decorated Chevalier in the Legion of Honor.

April 28–29, 1996
Premiere of the documentary *Visages de la Shoah* and Marcel Jabelot's classroom visits, at the Agnes Irwin School (Rosemont, Pennsylvania).

March 23, 1999
Death of Marcel Jabelot.

**Marcel Jabelot in his apartment in
Neuilly-sur-Seine.**
© Evvy Eisen, The Legacy Project

Rue de Rivoli, 1944. BHVP

COMPREHENSION QUESTIONS

PART ONE

1) THE GERMAN OCCUPATION

What do we learn about Marcel Jabelot and his family? Why did they, like many other Jewish families, leave Paris? Explain the difference between the Occupied Zone and the Free Zone.

2) THE ARREST OF MARCEL JABELOT

With whom was Monsieur Jabelot arrested? How does he explain the fact that the Gestapo knew how and where to find the Jews?

3) DRANCY

Describe life in the Drancy internment camp. Where was it located? Why is it often called the "anti-chamber of death" or the "anti-chamber of Auschwitz"?

4) THE TRAIN TO AUSCHWITZ

How were conditions in the train to Poland? What did the Jewish deportees think, and how did the Nazis try to reassure them?

5) ARRIVAL AT AUSCHWITZ

What happened when the train stopped at Auschwitz-Birkenau? What did the Nazis instruct the Jews to do?

6) TATTOOING A NUMBER

How did the Germans humiliate the Jewish prisoners?

7) THE FIRST NIGHT

What were the sleeping arrangements at Auschwitz-Birkenau? And what did the Germans do the first night?

8) THE FOOD

Describe the food at Auschwitz and the effect it had on nineteen-year-old Marcel Jabelot.

9) BIRKENAU

What happened to the women who were deported with Jabelot, including his mother and grandmother? How can you explain the fact that certain deportees were gassed upon arrival at Auschwitz-Birkenau?

10) THE COAL MINE

Where were Marcel and his father sent? For what reason? What was the hardest part for young Jabelot?

11) THE BELGIAN ARCHITECT

What role did the Belgian architect play in Jabelot's survival? And why was this gentleman reasonably well-treated by the Germans?

12) THE DEATH MARCH

Why did the Germans evacuate the camps in January 1945 and force the prisoners to walk? How did most of the Jews die? What were the conditions? And how did Jabelot survive?

13) THE POLISH WOMAN

How did the Polish lady help Jabelot and the other survivors of the Death March? Why was it dangerous for her?

14) THE RUSSIANS

How was Jabelot helped by the Russians? And why couldn't he return to France at that time?

15) THE RED CROSS

What advice did Jabelot receive from the Red Cross volunteer? And how did he manage to get to Rumania?

16) BUCAREST-ODESSA-MARSEILLE

Why was Jabelot eager to return to France? How did he get to Marseille in May 1945?

17) THE POST-WAR PERIOD

What did Jabelot find when he returned to Paris? How did he learn that no one else in his family had survived? How was he treated for tuberculosis?

18) ANTI-SEMITISM

How does Jabelot explain the fact that most French people did nothing to help the Jews in the early years of the War? And how did things change somewhat in 1943? Who else, according to Jabelot, must take responsibility for the fate of the Jews?

PART TWO

19) RETURN TO PARIS

What difficulties confronted Jabelot when he returned to Paris? How does he explain the fact that he was somewhat able to put his life back together?

20) WORK

What type of business did Jabelot pursue after the War? What reason does he give for not returning to medical school?

21) THE SORBONNE

Why did Jabelot retire at sixty and become a student at the Sorbonne? What questions did he ask? And did he find the answers?

22) LOSS OF FAITH

After Auschwitz, why was it so difficult for Jabelot to believe in God? How did his feelings change toward his fellow man?

23) MARRIAGE

Why did Jabelot hesitate to get married? Why did he feel lucky to meet Danièle Leclercq?

24) BEARING WITNESS

Why is it so important for Jabelot to tell his story? How do young people react to his testimony?

25) LESSONS

What advice does Jabelot give to young people? What must they do to avoid dictatorship and discrimination?

DISCUSSION QUESTIONS

1) Why do you think that most French people did little to help the Jews in the beginning of the War? How and why did attitudes change?

2) Many French people collaborated with the Germans and denounced Jews. Why do you think that was the case?

3) Describe all that the Nazis did to the Jews in the concentration camps.

4) Imagine that you are the Polish woman who helped Jabelot and his comrades. Explain what risks you were taking and why you chose to help the escaped prisoners.

5) Discuss the question of "friendship" in Jabelot's testimony. Where do we see the existence of these ties and how did they help Jabelot survive?

6) Jabelot often says that he was lucky. Do you agree with him? Explain.

7) Imagine that you are Jabelot in the Egersfeld Forest. Nearly all of your comrades were machine-gunned by the Nazis. What were your thoughts and feelings? And how did you decide to remain still?

8) Describe the anti-Semitism in France before and during the War.

9) Explain how Jabelot created a new life for himself after the War.

10) Do you find it understandable that Marcel Jabelot lost faith in man and in God after Auschwitz? Explain.

11) How could following Jabelot's advice make the world a better place?

12) Write a letter to Marcel Jabelot. Share with him your thoughts and feelings about what he experienced.

RECOMMENDED BIBLIOGRAPHY

HISTORY

Adler, Jacques. *The Jews of Paris and the Final Solution.* Oxford: Oxford University Press, 1987.

Bower, Tom. *Klaus Barbie: The Butcher of Lyons.* New York: Pantheon Books, 1984.

Braunschweig, Maryvonne and Bernard Gidel. *Les Déportés d'Avon: Au Revoir les Enfants.* Paris: La Découverte, 1989.

Cohen, Richard I. *The Burden of Conscience: French Jewry's Response to the Holocaust.* Bloomington: Indiana University Press, 1987.

Colombat, André Pierre. *The Holocaust in French Film.* Metuchen, New Jersey & London: The Scarecrow Press, Inc., 1993.

Dank, Milton. *The French against the French.* Philadelphia: J.B. Lippincott, 1974.

Epstein, Eric Joseph and Philip Rosen. *Dictionary of the Holocaust: Biography, Geography and Terminology.* Westport: Greenwood Press, 1997.

Gildea, Robert. *Marianne in Chains: Daily Life in the Heart of France during the German Occupation.* New York: Metropolitan Books, 2002.

Jackson, Julian. *France: The Dark Years, 1940–1944.* Oxford: Oxford University Press, 2001.

Klarsfeld, Serge, Susan Cohen, Howard M. Epstein and Glorianne Depondt. *French Children of the Holocaust: A Memorial*. New York: NYU Press, 1996.

Klarsfeld, Serge. *Memorial to the Jews Deported from France 1942–1944*. New York: Beate Klarsfeld Foundation, 1983.

Lanzmann, Claude. *Shoah: An Oral History of the Holocaust*. New York: Pantheon, 1987.

Latour, Amy. *The Jewish Resistance in France*. New York: Holocaust Library, 1981.

Lévy, Claude and Paul Tillard. *Betrayal at the Vél d'Hiv*. Preface by Joseph Kessel. Translated by Inea Bushnaq. New York: Hill and Wang, 1969.

Maurrus, Michael R. and Robert O. Paxton. *Vichy France and the Jews*. Stanford: Stanford University Press, 1981.

Ousby, Ian. *Occupation: The Ordeal of France 1940–1944*. New York: St. Martin's Press, 1998.

Paxton, Robert O. *Vichy France: Old Guard and New Order, 1940-1944*. New York: Columbia University Press, 1972.

Sweets, John F. *Choices in Vichy France: The French Under the Nazi Occupation*. Oxford: Oxford University Press, 1994.

Weisberg, Richard H. *Vichy Law and the Holocaust in France*. New York: New York University Press, 1996.

Zuccotti, Susan. *The Holocaust, the French, and the Jews*. New York: Basic Books, 1993.

MEMOIRS AND LITERARY WORKS

Aubrac, Lucie. *Outwitting the Gestapo.* Translated by Konrad Bieber. Lincoln: University of Nebraska Press, 1993.

Barnett, Barbara P. *Visages de la Shoah : Marcel Jabelot.* Wayne, Pennsylvania: Beach Lloyd Publishers, 2004.

Cretzmeyer, Stacy. *Your Name is Renée.* New York: Oxford University Press, 1999.

Delbo, Charlotte. *Convoy to Auschwitz: Women of the French Resistance.* Translated by Carol Cosman. Boston: Northeastern University Press, 1997.

Delbo, Charlotte. *None of Us Will Survive.* Boston: Beacon Press, 1968.

Fry, Varian. *Surrender on Demand.* Boulder, Colorado: Johnson Books, 1997.

Hallie, Philip P. *Lest Innocent Blood Be Shed.* New York: Harper and Row, 1979.

Idrac, Armand. *Memoirs from Normandy: Childhood, War & Life's Adventures.* Translated & edited by Joanne Silver. Wayne, Pennsylvania: Beach Lloyd Publishers, 2004.

Idrac, Armand. *Drôle de Mémoires en Normandie. Avant-propos par Emmanuel Le Roy Ladurie.* Wayne, Pennsylvania: Beach Lloyd Publishers, 2004.

Joffo, Joseph. *A Bag of Marbles.* Translated by Martin Sokolinsky. Boston: Houghton Mifflin Co, 1974.

Roth-Hano, Renee. *Touch Wood: A Girlhood in Occupied France.* New York: Puffin Books, 1989.

Tichauer, Eva. *I Was # 20832 at Auschwitz.* Translated by Colette Lévy and Nicki Rensten. London: Vallentine Mitchell, 2000.

Wiesel, Elie. *Night.* New York: Hill and Wang-Avon Books, 1972.

INTERNET RESOURCES

(Accessed and verified August 14–15, 2004)

Anti-Defamation League. www.adl.org

Beach Lloyd Publishers, LLC. www.beachlloyd.com

Centre de documentation juive contemporaine.
www.Memorial-cdjc.org

The Chambon Foundation.
www.chambon.org/chambon_foundation_en.htm

Facing History and Ourselves. www.facing.org

La France Divisée. www.francedivided.com

History Learning Site. www.historylearningsite.co.uk

Holocaust Teacher Resource Center. www.holocaust-trc.org

Mémorial de Caen — Histoire pour la Paix.
www.Unicaen.fr/collectivite/memorial

Simon Wiesenthal Center. www.wiesenthal.com

United States Holocaust Memorial Museum.
 www.ushmm.org

Yad Vashem. www.yadvashem.org

INDEX

ABOUT THE AUTHOR

Photo by Harry Hartz

Barbara P. Barnett, teacher of French and Head of the Department of Modern Languages at The Agnes Irwin School in Rosemont, Pennsylvania, has spent nearly a decade interviewing French Holocaust survivors, Hidden Children, Christians who risked their lives to help Jews, historians and members of the Resistance. The recipient of several teaching grants for her work, Barnett has conducted research in France and in the United States. Her work currently includes speaking at professional conferences and conducting teacher workshops.

ADDITIONAL WORKS BY THE AUTHOR

Visages de la Shoah : Marcel Jabelot.
The original French version of this book, suitable for intermediate and/or advanced readers.

Faces of the Holocaust: Marcel Jabelot.
The sixty-minute, award-winning documentary in VHS or DVD formats; in French, available with or without English sub-titles.

CONTACT BEACH LLOYD PUBLISHERS, LLC

LLC

Web: http://www.BEACHLLOYD.com
E-mail: BEACHLLOYD@erols.com
Phone: (610) 407-0130 or
Toll-free: 1-866-218-3253, Ext. 8668
Fax: (775) 254-0633

P.O.Box 2183
Southeastern, PA 19399-2183

QUICK **Order Form**

🖶 **Fax orders**: 775-254-0633. Send this form.

☎ **Telephone orders**: Call 610-407-0130 or toll free 1-866-218-3253, Ext. 8668.

🖳 **E-mail orders**: BEACHLLOYD@erols.com

🖃 **Postal Orders**: Beach Lloyd Publishers, LLC
Joanne S. Silver, Mgr.
P.O. Box 2183
Southeastern PA 19399-2183
USA

Please send the following books & other products:

_____

_____

_____

Name: _____
Address: _____
City: _____ State: _____ ZIP: _____
Telephone: _____
E-mail address: _____

Sales tax: Please add 6% for products shipped to Pennsylvania addresses.

Shipping: **U.S.**: $2-4

International: $6-9; contact for estimate.

Payment: Check or Money Order in US dollars, payable to Beach Lloyd Publishers, LLC.

Visit www.BEACHLLOYD.com for products and pricing.